5-Minute

Minute

Pinkalicious

Stories

by Victoria Kann

HARPER

An Imprint of HarperCollinsPublishers

To Max
—V.K.

ISBN 978-0-06-256697-3

Typography by Kirsten Berger
18   19   20   21   LSCW   10 9 8 7 6 5 4

First Edition

Contents

Meet the Characters

The Pinkerton Family

Peter

Pinkalicious

Mommy

Daddy

Pinkalicious's Pals

Rose

Molly

Alison

Lila

Aqua

Goldilicious

Pinkalicious
Cherry Blossoms

I woke up one morning and couldn't believe my nose. I poked my head out the window and took a deep breath. I could smell it. I could feel it! There were butterflies and flowers everywhere. Spring was in the air!

This could mean only one thing. "Is it time for the Cherry Blossom Festival?" I asked.

"Tomorrow," Mommy said.

I danced around my bedroom. I couldn't wait. I loved seeing the trees in full bloom. I loved smelling their sweet scent. I loved watching the petals flutter to the ground. It was the pinkest day of the year!

"I'm going to fly a kite at the festival this year,"
I said. I showed Peter my pink cherry blossom kite.
"It will soar up and up in the sky next to the cherry
blossoms. It's going to be pinkatastic!"

Peter looked doubtful. "Do you know how to fly a kite?" he asked.

8

I shrugged. "I can try."

I practiced all day but had no luck at all!
I could not get my cherry blossom kite off
the ground. I couldn't believe it. The cherry
blossom festival wouldn't be the same
without my kite flying through the sky.

"Keep trying," Mommy said.
"Practice makes perfect."
I practiced and practiced. Mommy watched and gave me tips, but my kite wouldn't lift off the ground.

"Don't worry, Pinkalicious," Mommy said. "It's not very windy today. There's going to be a lot of wind at the festival tomorrow. You'll fly your kite then."

The next day, we skipped all the way to the festival.
I was wearing my special cherry blossom dress. "We're here!"
I cheered. The blossoms were more pinkatastic than ever!
A few petals fluttered to the ground. I took a deep breath.
The air smelled deliciously sweet. Once my kite was flying,
the festival would be perfect!

It was a very windy day, just like my mom had said. I
picked out a spot to fly my kite. "Here goes," I said.
I started to run.

There was a big gust of wind.

"That's it!" I yelled. "More wind! More!"

The breeze got stronger. Cherry blossoms swirled around me.

"Wait!" I said. "I can't see!"

The wind stopped blowing. The petals stopped swirling. I rubbed my eyes and blinked. I looked different. My special cherry blossom dress was gone. I was now wearing a pink silk dress with a yellow sash. Where was I?

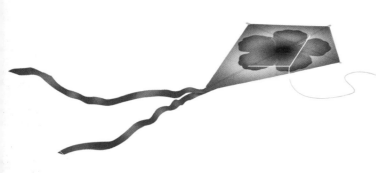

"Hello," said a girl. "I like your kimono." She pointed at my new pink dress. "My name is Sakura."

"I'm Pinkalicious," I said. "I like your kimono too." Sakura was wearing a yellow kimono with a purple sash.

"Come on," said Sakura. "The festival is starting soon! Can you help me hang these lanterns?"

Sakura picked up a lantern with a cherry blossom on it. "This one is like my name," she said. "Sakura means 'cherry blossom' in Japanese!"

I picked up a bright pink lantern. "This one makes me think of my name, too." I laughed.

Soon a parade went by. There were drums. There were dancers. There were colors everywhere! The women were wearing kimonos just like mine. They were also holding fans and umbrellas. "I love the umbrellas," I told Sakura. I pointed at a pink one. "That one is pink perfection!"

"That's a *wagasa*," Sakura said. "It's a traditional Japanese umbrella."

"Try some *mochi*," said Sakura. She gave me a pink rice cake filled with strawberry ice cream. I couldn't believe it. The *mochi* was almost as yummy as a cupcake!

I looked up at the sky
and spotted kites all around.
I got a little sad. I wished I
knew how to fly one.

"What's wrong,
Pinkalicious?" Sakura asked.

"I was hoping to fly a kite at the festival this year," I said.
"I practiced and I practiced, but my kite wouldn't fly."

Sakura understood. "Sometimes a friend can help," she
said. "I love flying kites." She picked up my kite. I held the
string. "Let's fly it together," Sakura said.

We ran together. There was a gust of wind. Sakura let go of the kite. It went up in the air! "Keep running!" she called. My legs went faster and faster. Suddenly, I was surrounded by a swirl of petals.

I was back in Pinkville. My kite was still flying! It flew up and up, past the cherry blossom trees. It was soaring high.

"Pinkalicious, you did it!" Mommy and Daddy cheered. "Look at that kite go!"

Peter looked surprised. "How did you get so good at this?" he asked.

I looked at my kite and smiled. "I got some help from a friend," I said. "Thank you, Sakura," I whispered.

Pinkalicious

Fashion Fun

Rose and Molly came over to play. Molly was holding a mysterious folder.

"What is in there?" I asked.

"They're pictures of designer clothing and fashion shows that I've collected from magazines," Molly explained.

"Those are beautiful outfits!" Rose said.

There were pink dresses and purple dresses. There were short dresses and dresses with flowy skirts. "I LOVE THESE DRESSES!" I said. "Look at this one! I think Mommy has a dress just like it. Let's look in her closet. We can try on her clothes and have our own fashion show!"

We went into Mommy's closet. It was full of beautiful
clothes! We took out skirts and shirts and shoes and dresses.
"This hat is so pretty!" Rose said.
"I like these shoes," I said.
"This scarf is very fashionable," Molly said.

Just then, Mommy came in. She did not look happy. "What are you girls doing?" Mommy asked. "That's my favorite scarf! My clothes are not for playtime!"

"We're fashion designers," I said. "Your clothes are like the ones in the magazine pictures! We're going to have a fashion show."

24

"That sounds like fun, Pinkalicious. Please use your imaginations, not my clothing," said Mommy.

"Ew, imaginary clothes!" said Rose. "How are we supposed to have a fashion show with those?"

Mommy laughed. "I think you can find a way. Now please play in your room, not my closet!" said Mommy.

Rose, Molly, and I sat on my bed. "I still want to have a fashion show," Molly said.

"Me too," I said. "But we don't have any fancy clothes!"

We looked at the pictures again. "I like those shoes with bows," I said. "I wish I had a pair."

"The bows look like pasta," said Molly.

She was right.

"I have an idea!" I said.

I told my friends my plan. It was going to take some work and we needed some supplies. "We need glue!" I said.

"Let's get twist ties!" said Rose.

"Don't forget glitter!" said Molly.

We gathered our supplies. My room became fashion headquarters. We cut and glued and glittered.

"What are you doing?"
asked Peter. "Can I do it, too?"

28

I thought about it. There was one thing that every fashion designer needed. "You can be a photographer," I said. "You can capture our designs on the runway!"

"Yes!" he yelled.

"Say cupcake and smile!"

I told Mommy about the idea. She agreed to help. The doorbell rang. My friends' mothers were here to pick them up. "Have a seat," said Mommy. "The girls have a surprise for you."

Mommy put down a long
rug. It was like a real runway!
    "Are you ready?" I asked my
friends. "It's show time!"

"Welcome to our fashion show!" Rose said as
we paraded into the living room.
    "We used things around the house to make
our clothes," I added.

"Look at my newspaper and coffee filter pants!" said Molly.

"My dress is made from Bubble Wrap!" I said.

Click! went Peter's camera.

"The flowers on my vest are cupcake liners," said Rose.

"What imaginative designs!" Mommy said. "You girls must have worked really hard."

"Bravo!" Rose's mommy cheered. "Show off your outfits and twirl!"

She didn't have to tell us twice. We twirled faster and faster!

Paper, ribbons, and cupcake liners went flying! Peter got closer and closer, trying to get the perfect picture. . .

POP, POP, POP, POP!

My dress was ruined! What a mess. How could I be a fashion designer without a design? I almost started to cry, but then I heard clapping!

"Marvelous!" Molly's mommy said. "You made a dress that can be worn two different ways, and now we can see your sparkly macaroni shoes!"

"Show off those shoes, Pinkalicious," Mommy said. "I love the pasta bows."

I held out one foot, then the other. "In the fashion world we call these a statement piece," I announced.

"Beautiful," Rose's mommy said. "If you stick with this," she said, "you'll have a career in fashion! I love how you used food in your designs."

"Oh yes!" I said. I was inspired.

I smiled and grabbed my sketchbook. I had an idea: a cupcake dress! I wonder if I could use real frosting.

Pinkalicious

and the Pink Parakeet

It was Bird Week at school, my favorite week ever! Ms. Penny had so much to teach us. Every day my class learned fun facts about birds.

I told my family everything I learned. "Fact," I told Mommy. "Hummingbirds can fly backwards."

"Fact," I told Daddy. "Robin eggs are blue."

"Fact," I told Peter. "Orioles can eat seventeen worms in a minute."

"Big whoop," he said. "So can I."

The last day of Bird Week was the best one. My class went on a field trip to the house of birds at the zoo. On the bus, I took out my bird book. There were pictures of every type of bird. There were small birds, like a sparrow, and big birds, like an eagle. There were a lot of fun facts, too. "Fact," I told Alison. "Parrots can talk like people."

I flipped through the pages of my book and saw something amazing. "Fact," I cried. "There's a pink parakeet! It's small and sweet and pinkerrifically pink!"

I showed the picture to Alison. "Wow," she said, "Look at its beautiful feathers."

"Yes," said Ms. Penny. "It's smart, too. But it's a very rare bird. You may not see one today."

I wasn't so sure about that. I was really good at bird-watching.

I spent the rest of the bus ride reading about the pink parakeet. Soon I was an expert! I was sure I could find a pink parakeet at the house of birds.

When we got to the house of birds, I couldn't believe my eyes. There were birds everywhere! I saw one red parrot, two blue peacocks, six green-and-yellow lovebirds, and a toucan with an orange beak. I did not see a single pink parakeet.

Alison and I admired the beautiful peacocks. We matched the parrot to the one in my bird book. We studied the toucan's beak and blew kisses at the lovebirds. It was a great field trip, but I still hadn't spotted a pink parakeet.

Soon it was time to leave. "I'm sorry, Pinkalicious," Alison said. "Maybe you'll see one another day."

We started walking out together, but just as we got to the door, I heard a strange call. "Pink, pink, pink, PINK!"

"What was that?" I said.

"Pink, pink, pink, PINK!"

Alison and I looked at each other. "The parrot!" we cried.

We ran over to the parrot's perch. "He's telling us something," I said. The parrot lifted its wing. It was pointing to the door. "Pink, pink, pink, PINK!" it called.

A pink parakeet! At last, I saw one. It was right inside Ms. Penny's hood!

"Wait, Ms. Penny!" I called, but she was already out the door.

By the time we caught up to Ms. Penny, it was too late.
Her hood was empty. The bird was gone.
    I was so upset. I told Ms. Penny what happened.
"Maybe it didn't fly far," she said. Together, the whole class
searched for the missing pink parakeet. Everyone scanned

the treetops, but the leaves were too thick. We looked
through the bushes, but we didn't see a thing. We looked
under benches and in the flower garden and along the path.
The pink bird wasn't anywhere.

I was about ready to give up. I took out my bird book and read about the pink parakeet again. That gave me an idea! I came up with a plan.

"Fact," I read out loud.

"'Pink Parakeets eat fruit.' Who has a snack?"

Molly had cherries from lunch. "You can use these, Pinkalicious," she said.

"Fact," I said. "'They also like taking baths.' How can we make a bath?"

"I know!" Jack filled a small dish with water. "A bird bath," he announced.

We put everything together. "I hope we find the pink parakeet," Alison said.

"Me too!" said Jack.

"There's one last fact," I said. "These parakeets tweet a lot. So here goes . . . !" I closed my eyes and thought pink thoughts. Then I whistled my very best pinkerrific birdcall.

Suddenly, I heard wings flapping. My classmates gasped. I opened my eyes, and there it was! The pink parakeet was eating fruit while taking a bath. It was as pinkerrific as its picture. The bird looked right at me. I whistled, and it tweeted back.

Ms. Penny laughed. "It looks like you made a new friend, Pinkalicious," she said.

Ms. Penny picked up the parakeet gently. "This is a really rare bird," she told the class. "We're lucky we get to see it." Everyone gathered around to get a better look. "Now it's time to take this bird home," Ms. Penny said, and she brought it back to the birdhouse. The whole class cheered!

When she came back, Ms. Penny laughed.
"Pinkalicious saved the day," she said.
"And that's a fact!"

Pinkalicious

and the Sick Day

When the bell rang at the end of the day, Principal Hart handed me a letter. "Give this to your mom," she said. "It's very important!"

Uh-oh. Was I in trouble?

When I got home, I found Mommy.
I waited while she read the letter.
I was nervous. "Did I do something
wrong?" I asked.

"No. You did something great." Mommy smiled. "You have perfect attendance. Tomorrow you get to be principal for the day," she said. "I'm very proud of you!"

"Yippee!" I yelled. "I'm in charge. No homework! Cupcakes for lunch!"

"I don't know about that," Mommy said. "However, you do get to read the morning announcements and eat lunch with Principal Hart. It will be a special day!"

"I can't wait!" I said.

After dinner, I worked on my announcer's voice. It had to be loud and clear, so the whole school could hear me.

"What will you say, Pinkalicious?" Mommy asked.

"Pinkawelcome, pupils of Pinkville!" I said in my best announcer's voice. Hmmm, too many words beginning with the letter *P*. I should keep it simple. How about:

"Good morning, students," I said. "Principal Pinkalicious here!"

"Too boring," Peter said.

I tried once more. "Good morning, this is Principal Pinkalicious, wishing you a pinkatastic day!"

Peter clapped. "I like it!"

"Bravo, Pinkalicious," Daddy said. "That sounds perfect. You must be very excited. Your cheeks are all pink."

I nodded. I was excited, but my throat felt weird.
"I think I practiced too much," I said.
"You need a good night's sleep,"
Mommy told me. She was right. I was
also very sleepy. I went to bed early.

When I woke, my head hurt. My eyes itched. My throat felt scratchy. *Achoo! Achoo! Achoo!*

"Are you okay, Pinkalicious?" Mommy asked.

"I don't feel so good," I said.

Daddy took my temperature. "You have a fever," he said. "No school for you today." He tucked me back into bed.

Then I remembered. "I HAVE to go to school," I said. "I'm principal for the day!"

"I'm sorry, Pinkalicious," Mommy said. "You need to rest up and get better."

I couldn't believe it. I was supposed to be Principal Pinkalicious, the most pinkerrific principal the school had ever seen. My big day was ruined.

"I will make you some tea," said Mommy.

Daddy tried to cheer me up. He put my favorite books on my bed. "Feel better, Pinkalicious," he said. Then he gave me a big hug, and I went back to sleep.

I woke up feeling a bit better, but I still had the sniffles. I looked in the mirror. My nose was perfectly pink!

Mommy came in with pink tea. "My mom used to make this for me when I was sick," she said. "It's elderberry tea." I took a sip. "Yum!" Mommy and I drank our tea together. "I've never had a tea party in bed!" I said.

I got to stay in my pajamas all day! Mommy brought me crayons, and I colored in bed. I drew a picture of me riding Goldie to school. It made me sad to think of school, so I drew another picture of Goldie. This time, she was taking a big jump, with me on her back!

Daddy called from work to see how I was. He told me a joke to make me laugh. "Why did the pink panda go to the doctor's office? Because she was pink!" I giggled, but I was still a little sad because I wasn't at school. I would not be able to share the joke at recess.

In the afternoon, the phone rang. It was Principal Hart!
"I'm home sick, too," she said. "When you come back,
you can still be principal for the day." I felt a pinka-million
times better.

Then Peter came home. "The announcements were boring today," he told me. "I missed Principal Pinkalicious!"

"Don't worry," I told him. "Principal Pinkalicious will come to the rescue tomorrow!"

That made Peter happy.

65

"Guess what I did today?" I said. "I colored and I read books. Mommy made me pink tea, and we had a tea party in bed, and I didn't even have to get dressed!"

"I want to be sick, too! " said Peter. Then he smelled my cold medicine. "Yuck, forget it!" he said. I giggled.

The next morning, my nose was a normal color and I felt all better.

"Your temperature is normal," Mommy said. "You can go to school today."

"Yay!" I cheered.

When I got to school, I went straight to the office. I couldn't wait to tell everyone the joke about the pink panda! "Good morning," I said. "This is Principal Pinkalicious!"

Pinkalicious
Story Time

We were at a book fair, waiting in line. I was going to meet my hero, Princess Plum! I have all her books.

Meet the Author of the Princess Plum books.

Princess Plum is kind. She is smart. She grants magic wishes and wears a sparkly purple tiara. I love her stories. In my favorite one, she turns a little girl into a princess for a day. The girl even gets to wear Princess Plum's tiara. I wish I could be princess for a day! But meeting Princess Plum is almost as good.

"I hope she signs my book," I told Mommy. "And lets me try on her tiara!" I couldn't believe I was going to meet a real princess at last.

But when we got to the front of the line, I was very surprised. Instead of a princess, I saw a man! He had gray hair and a gray beard, and no tiara at all.

"Hello," he said. "Are you a fan of Princess Plum?"

I nodded. "I want to be just like her," I said.

"I always love meeting my fans," the man said. "Would you like me to sign your book?"

I was very confused. "Is Princess Plum a man?" I said.

"I'm Syd Silver." The man laughed. "I'm the author of Princess Plum. That means I write books about her."

"You wrote all the books about her?" I asked.

"Every single one," said Mr. Silver.

"But how can you write about being a magic princess if you aren't one?" I asked.

"When you're an author, you can tell all sorts of stories," said Mr. Silver. "Princess Plum is a character I made up. Stories can be about anyone or anything you want. Just use your imagination!"

That afternoon, I couldn't stop thinking about what Mr. Silver had said. I had a great imagination! I decided to give it a try. I imagined I could fly and wrote about soaring above Pinkville. Down below, the houses were miniature and the cars looked like toys. In my story, I made the clouds into cotton candy.

After that, I wrote about a tea party with dancing spoons and cups.

I wrote about a garden growing under my bed.

I wrote about a family of pirates that lived inside the washing machine. They sailed on a miniature boat and hunted for treasure in our laundry.

I couldn't stop writing! At dinnertime, I wrote about a broccoli jungle and sweet-potato mountains. At bedtime, I curled up under my blanket and wrote by the light of a flashlight. I wrote about a pair of bunny slippers hopping all over the house. They hopped from my closet into the living room and all the way out to the backyard!

At school on Monday, I came up with more ideas. I wrote them all down. I was too busy to listen to my teacher, Ms. Penny. There were so many stories to write! I was writing about a pink panda when Ms. Penny tapped my shoulder. "Pinkalicious," she said. "What are you doing?"

I gulped. I told Ms. Penny everything, about meeting the author Syd Silver and how he was the one who wrote the stories about Princess Plum. Then I told her that I'd been writing my own stories all day long. "I'm sorry for not paying attention," I said.

"Well," said Ms. Penny, "paying attention is very important. But so is being creative. I think I have an idea."

"Listen everybody," said Ms. Penny. "This week, you are all going to be authors! We will have special writing time so you can work on your stories. And on Friday, we'll have our own class book festival."

I was so excited. I was going to be a real author, just like Syd Silver!

At recess, we talked about our ideas. "I'm writing about a penguin named Percy," said Molly.

"I'm writing about a family of giants who live in the rain forest," said Rose.

Alison's book was the biggest surprise. It didn't have any words! She was making a comic-book story with only pictures.

We worked hard all week. I finished the story about
flying through the cotton-candy clouds. In the story,
I flew up above the trees, higher than
the butterflies, alongside the
birds. I flew faster and faster.
The clouds were soft
against my arms.

I drew the cover and added an "about the author" page. "Pinkalicious is from Pinkville," I wrote. "She loves writing, baking cupcakes, and anything pink!"

On Friday, we read our stories out loud. Alison went first. I read my story next. I loved listening to my classmates' stories. They were all very different. "Who knew we had such great imaginations in our class?" Ms. Penny said.

We signed our books, just like Mr. Silver had done. I felt like a real author. It was so much fun!

"I loved your story, Pinkalicious," said Alison.

"I want to hear it again!" said Rose.

So I read my story one more time for my friends.

Before I went home, I told Ms. Penny I had one last thing to write.

Dear Mr. Silver,
You may not be a princess who grants wishes, but your books are full of magic. Thank you for helping me see that I am a writer too!

Pinkalicious

Pinkalicious

Tutu-rrific

Alison and I giggled as we tried to balance on our toes. Alison pointed one foot out behind her. "This is called an arabesque," she told me. "It's my favorite dance move."

"Look!" I pointed my foot behind me. "I'm doing it!"

Tomorrow we were going to ballet class together! I was pink with glee.

I had never taken a ballet class before, but Alison had. "You'll love it," she said. "We twirl and jump through the air and spin on our tippy-toes. We even do pirouettes," Alison said. She put her hands above her head and did a beautiful spin.

"What fun!" I said. "I can't wait to dance."

"Plus we get to dress like real ballerinas," Alison told me.

"What's your outfit like?" I asked.

"It's a purple tutu with purple slippers," said Alison. "What does yours look like?"

I laughed and said, "Guess!"

The next day, I got ready: I wore my pink tutu, pink slippers, and pink bows in my hair. Alison was right. I looked like a real ballerina! I couldn't wait to dance like one, too.

Mommy took me to class. When we got there, I thought
I saw a purple tutu. "There's Alison!" I said. I said bye to
Mommy and ran inside to catch Alison.

"Have fun!" Mommy called after me. The ballet school was
crowded. There were people all over! I thought I saw a flash
of purple run into a room.

"Alison, wait!" I called. But Alison didn't hear me. I followed her into the class. There were tutus of every color. Orange tutus and yellow tutus and blue tutus! But I didn't see Alison. I couldn't spot her with all the dancers.

Just then, the teacher walked in. She was wearing a
beautiful green tutu. "Okay, everyone!" she said. "Take your
place at the barre." I'd have to find Alison later. It was time
for my very first ballet class!

"Time to warm up," said the teacher. "First position," she called. I looked around the room. Everyone was moving their feet. Heels together, toes apart. I did it, too. This was easy!

"The plié," the teacher sang. The ballerinas bent their knees, so I did, too. Piece of cake!

"Very good," said the teacher. "Now, let's go over the dance we learned last week." I didn't know the moves, but I wasn't worried. Ballet seemed really, really simple. The teacher put on some music. The dancers moved their arms, first up, then down. Then they kicked their legs up and down. I followed along just fine. Suddenly, the music got faster. The girls skipped in a circle and jumped in the air. I was stuck in the middle, not sure what to do.

Everyone moved so quickly. I couldn't keep up! When I hopped, they kicked. When I kicked, they swayed. "Time for the grand jeté!" the teacher called. The girls all leaped into the air. How did they know so many moves?

"Hold on!" I cried. But no one could hear me. I looked around for Alison, but she wasn't there. It was a girl who looked like Alison. I had made a mistake.

I knew I had to say something. I stopped dancing and raised my hand. "Excuse me," I said. "I think I'm in the wrong class!" Just as I put my hand up, the dancers jumped up high again.

"Beautiful!" said the teacher. She didn't see me!

I tried to get out of the circle, but the dancers linked arms. I tried crawling through their legs, but the dancers hopped up and down. I saw silky ballet slippers everywhere I looked. "Wait!" I shouted, but nothing helped. I was trapped between tutus with no way out.

"Get ready for the grand finale!" the teacher called out. The girls spread out their arms and started twirling.

"Oh!" I said, happily surprised. I could do this! I took a deep breath and twirled and whirled and spun around. I did a pirouette just like Alison. I was doing it! I was a real ballerina. I was spinning so freely, I didn't notice that everyone had stopped. They were all watching me.

The teacher looked at me, confused. "You!" she said. "You're not in this class!"

"Uh-oh," I whispered. I was sure I was in trouble.

Instead, the teacher just smiled. "You must be in the wrong room," she said. "I'll have someone walk you to the beginner class. But first, could you spin again?"

I twirled around once more. "You're so graceful!" said the teacher. "Keep practicing and soon you will be in my advanced class."

An older girl walked me to my class. "Have fun," she said. "And keep twirling!"

In the beginner class, I told Alison what happened. "The teacher said I was graceful!" I said proudly.

"Wow, I can't believe you danced in an advanced class. What was it like?" Alison asked.

"It was tutu-rrific!" I said, and did a pirouette.

Pinkalicious
and Planet Pink

In science class, we learned about the planets. They are the most amazing things in the world. I mean, the universe!

"Every planet has its own color," said Ms. Penny. "Earth is blue and green. Mars is a deep shade of red. Venus is bright and milky white."

Ms. Penny showed us something I'll never forget. "There's even a pink planet," she said. "Scientists just discovered it. They don't know much about it yet."

I couldn't believe it. "What's it called?" I asked.

"It doesn't have a real name yet," said Ms. Penny.

"I'll call it Planet Pink!" I said. "The most pinkerrific planet in the universe!"

Our Solar System

Mercury Venus Earth Mars Jupiter Saturn

For homework, we had to imagine what the pink planet is like. I had lots of ideas. I know a thing or two about pink places, after all.

I made a list. *Looks like a giant pink gumball, full of glittery stardust, home to fuzzy pink aliens called Pinktonians.* Then I took out my pink paint to make a picture of Planet Pink.

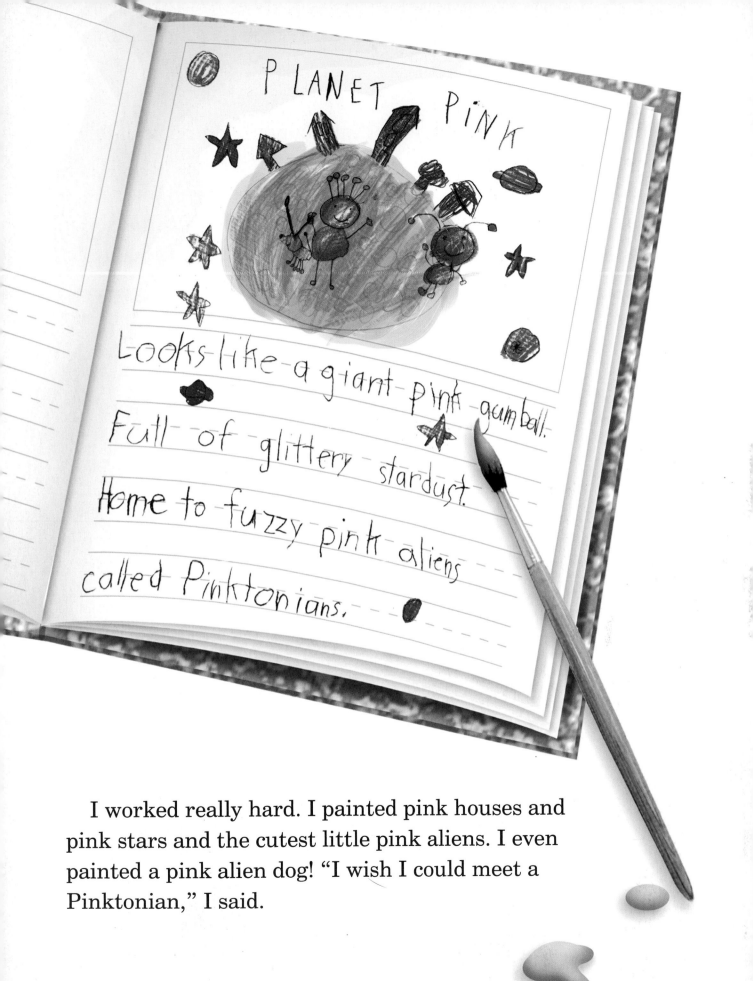

PLANET PINK

Looks like a giant pink gumball.
Full of glittery stardust.
Home to fuzzy pink aliens
called Pinktonians.

I worked really hard. I painted pink houses and
pink stars and the cutest little pink aliens. I even
painted a pink alien dog! "I wish I could meet a
Pinktonian," I said.

"There's no such thing as a Pinktonian," Peter said later, when I showed him my work.

"How do you know?" I said. "Have you ever seen one?"

Peter thought it over. "No," he replied. "I don't think so." Then he got very excited at the thought of meeting an alien.

"Maybe Pinktonians will come to Earth!" cried Peter. "They'll fly down in their spaceship. When they land, they'll say, "Take me to Peter!"

"No way," I said. "If Pinktonians come to visit, they'll want to meet me first. I'm the most pinkerrific, pink-loving person on the planet!"

"Maybe they'll like you so much," said Peter, "they'll want to take you back home with them."

"Ha-ha-ha," I said.
I knew Peter was
just teasing.

That night, I had a weird dream. A beam of light
shone in my window. I followed the bright pink footsteps.
There, in my yard, was a huge pink spaceship next to a
tiny pink alien! I recognized that alien. It looked just like
the ones in my drawing!

"Greetings," said the alien. "I am a Pinktonian. You may
call me Pinky."

"Hello," I said shyly. I couldn't believe I was face-to-face with a real live Pinktonian.

"We have come to take you to Planet Pink," said Pinky. "We hear you make great cupcakes. They are our favorite food."

Pinky seemed nice, and the offer was exciting. Planet Pink *was* the most pinkerrific planet in the universe, after all. But I didn't want to leave home. The more I thought about it, the more upset I got. "Please don't make me go," I said. "Noooo, I want to stay here!"

Just then, I woke up.
I wasn't in my front yard next to a spaceship. I was in my bed, holding my teddy bear. I was safe and sound.

Except…something was odd.

There *was* a beam of light coming through my window. And all over the floor were bright pink footprints!

I ran to get Peter. "Wake up!" I cried. "There's a Pinktonian in my room!" I told him my dream. I showed him the clues.

Peter grabbed a flashlight. I grabbed my wand. We both put on our exploring hats. We tiptoed around the room looking for the alien. Suddenly, we heard a scratch. Then we heard a screech. Then we saw something moving under my bed. My bedspread flapped. My bedspread fluttered. "IT'S THE ALIEN!" we shouted. We went running toward the door.

We ran straight into Mommy and Daddy. They turned on the lights. "What's going on here?" they asked.

"There is an alien from Planet Pink under my bed!" I cried. There was another scratch. My bedspread flapped some more.

Mommy knelt down.

"Do you see it?" I asked. "It's fuzzy and pink and has three antennas!"

Mommy started laughing. "Look, Pinkalicious." There *was* a creature down there. But instead of a pink alien, it was a fuzzy white kitty!

"It's the neighbor's new cat," said Mommy. She must have climbed in the window and stepped in your pink paint. I'll wipe off her paws."

I knelt down to pet the kitty. "Hello," I said.

"Meow," the kitty said back.

"I think she likes you, Pinkalicious," Daddy said.

"We'll take her home tomorrow. Good night, space explorers," said Daddy.

I got under the covers. The kitty snuggled up beside me.
I hadn't met a Pinktonian, but I'd made a new friend.

As I drifted off to sleep, I saw the kitten's collar.
Her name was Luna, which is another word for the moon!
How pinkaperfect!

Pinkalicious
The Royal Tea Party

Goldilicious is the best unicorn ever! She's smart and kind and a great friend. She even lets me ride her whenever I want. Goldilicious is golderrific, and I want everyone to know it.

"I want to show Goldilicious how special she is," I told Peter.

"You should throw her a party," Peter said. "You can give her the royal treatment!"

That gave me a great idea. "Listen, Goldie," I said. (Goldie is her nickname.) "I'm going to crown you Princess Goldilicious."

There was a LOT to do to get ready for the coronation.

I got my special tea set out. No coronation is complete without a royal tea party! "Can I do something?" Peter asked.

"Sorry, Peter," I said. "This party is only for members of the royal court."

"I want to be in the royal court," Peter begged. "There must be something I can do!"

I thought about what Peter does the best. Peter likes to eat. "Maybe you could be the royal taster," I said. "That means you taste all the food to make sure it's perfect."

"Great idea," Peter said. "I'll be the best taster this royal court has ever seen. I can't wait to start!"

I decorated the backyard with Goldie's favorite color: PINK! I put out a pink picnic blanket and hung a garland of pink flowers on the fence. I even added pink bows. The backyard had never looked better.

Then I went inside and planned the perfect menu. There would be tea and sandwiches and cookies and cupcakes. I wanted everything to be extra perfect for Goldilicious.

I brought a cup of tea out to my royal taster. "What do you think, Peter?" I asked.

Peter had a little sip of tea. "This tastes okay," Peter said. "It's a little boring, though."

"Don't be silly," I told him. "It's perfect! It's tea fit for royalty."

Soon my guests arrived. "Come in, come in!" I cried. "You're just in time to help get Goldie ready. We need to brush her mane and shine her horn. And of course, every princess needs her royal sash."

"Can I help?" Peter asked. "I bet I'm really good with sashes."

"No, thanks," I said. "But you can go to the kitchen and take the food outside."

Peter went into the kitchen.
He was in there for a long time.
"What are you doing in there?"
I called. "The royal taster is only
supposed to have *one* taste!"

"I'm just making sure the food
is perfect," Peter replied. "I'm coming
outside now."

Finally, Goldie was ready. "Let the royal tea party begin!" I declared.

My friends and I sat down. Goldie had the place of honor. I noticed that the food looked a little different.

I sipped my tea. "Pardon me a moment," I said to my guests. Then I dragged Peter away. "What did you do to the tea?" I whispered.

"I made it better," Peter said. "I used all my favorite foods. I put maple syrup in one teacup. I added peanut butter to another. I stirred strawberry jam and vanilla yogurt into the other teacups," Peter continued.

"As the royal taster, I felt the sandwiches were tasteless, so I made better ones with ice cream instead of mayonnaise and goldfish crackers instead of tuna fish."

"This is a disaster!" I cried. "My royal taster has turned into a royal pain!"

I went back to apologize to my guests. "Please excuse the food," I said. "My royal taster did NOT follow directions." But my friends were so busy eating that they didn't hear me.

"Yum!" Molly exclaimed. "This sandwich is delicious! It's sweet and salty."

"My tea tastes yummy, too," Lila added. "I've never had tea like this before. What's your secret, Pinkalicious?"

I tasted my tea again. It tasted like maple syrup—Hmm, it *was* good!

My friends didn't seem to mind. The food tasted extra special. Maybe this party wasn't a disaster after all. Maybe it was . . .

A perfect royal tea party!

"Let the coronation begin!" I said. Goldie pranced forward. "Goldilicious, you are the smartest, most beautiful unicorn ever. I'm so lucky to have you as my friend." I touched my wand to Goldie's horn. "I hereby royally declare you Princess Goldilicious!" I said.

"I have something for you, too," I told Peter. I gave Peter a new hat. It was a special white chef's hat. Then I touched my wand to his head. "And I declare YOU Sir Peter the Chef!" I said.

"Hear, hear!" said Peter. "Who wants more?"

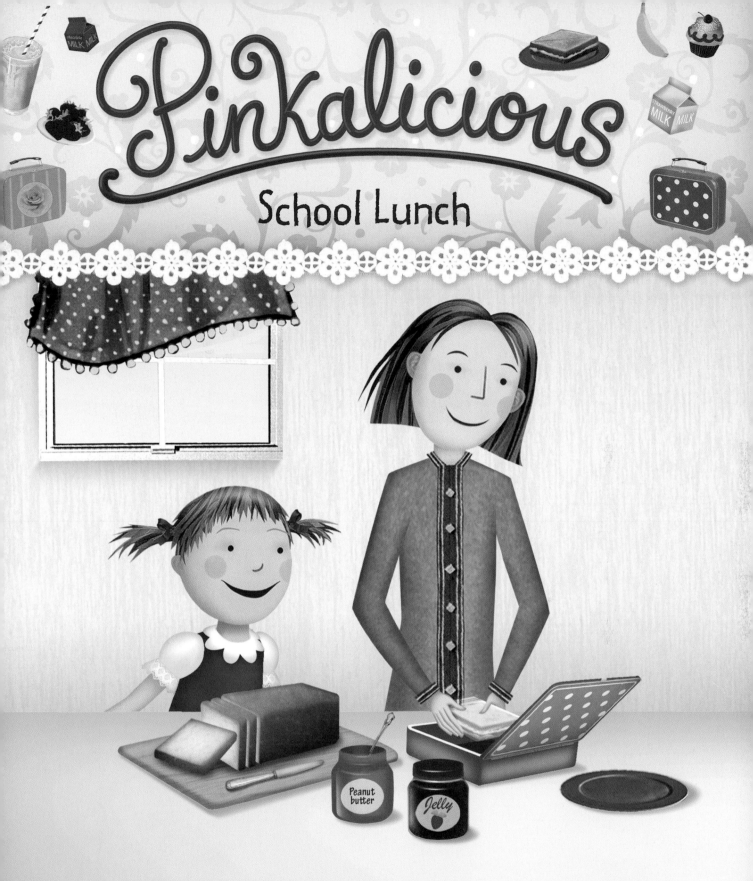

Pinkalicious

School Lunch

If there's one thing I love for lunch, it's a peanut butter and jelly sandwich. Mommy packs it for me almost every day.

On Monday, I decided to try something totally different. I wanted to buy my lunch at the school cafeteria. It would be pinkerrific! They were serving spaghetti and meatballs with raspberry Jell-O for dessert. (Spaghetti looks pink if you use your imagination.)

MENU

Spaghetti and Meatballs

Salad

Strawberry milk

Raspberry Jell-O

Chocolate milk

At last, the bell rang.

"Lunchtime!" I yelled.

I leaped out of my seat and out the door, skipping down the hall at full speed. I was going so fast I didn't see the book on the floor. I tripped and fell and hurt my knee.

Ms. Penny came to help me. "Why the rush, Pinkalicious?" she asked.

I told her about the spaghetti and meatballs and pink Jell-O for dessert. "Sounds yummy," she said. "But remember, slow and steady wins the race." I wasn't sure what she meant, but I was too hungry to ask.

Ms. Penny walked down to the cafeteria with me. I got in line and waved good-bye. Soon enough, my special spaghetti would be all mine! All I had to do now was wait.

So I waited. And waited. And waited.

The line was so long it snaked around the cafeteria. We moved slowly, inch by inch. My tummy started grumbling. My knee throbbed. The room was noisier than I remembered. This was taking forever!

At long last, it was my turn to order. I cleared my throat and said, "Spaghetti and meatballs with raspberry Jell-O, please!"

Ethel the lunch lady didn't hear me.

"Excuse me?" she said.

"Spaghetti and meatballs and Jell-O," I tried again.

It was no use. The room was too loud. Ethel shrugged and handed me a plate with green beans and a sloppy joe. No matter how hard I squinted, it did not look pink—or tasty.

I cleared my throat to try one last time, but just then, the bell rang. It was time to go back to class!

I couldn't believe what just happened. This was supposed to be my big day, my cafeteria feast! Now instead of spaghetti and meatballs and raspberry Jell-O, I had nothing but an empty stomach.

In math class, I had trouble paying attention. I was so hungry!

Triangles looked like pizza slices. Circles looked like pies.

When Ms. Penny showed us that a square cut diagonally makes two triangles, I thought she was cutting a sandwich in half.

My tummy grumbled.

That night, I told Mommy and Daddy about how everything had gone wrong: how I had tripped and fallen, how I had hurt my knee, how it had taken forever to get through the line, and how when I finally got there, the lunch lady couldn't hear my order.

"I'm sorry, honey," said Daddy.

"Would you like me to make you a peanut butter and jelly sandwich for tomorrow?" asked Mommy.

I didn't know what to do. Today did not turn out very well, but tomorrow they were serving grilled-cheese sandwiches. I like grilled cheese!

"I'll try again tomorrow, except this time, I'll be prepared," I said.

I finished my dinner and went up to my room. If I was going to actually eat the school lunch, I needed to have a plan.

The next day at school, when the lunch bell rang, I pulled out the plan I had made the night before.

"'Step one,'" I read out loud, "'watch your pace! Slow and steady wins the race.'" I made sure not to rush to the cafeteria, and this time, I made it without falling or bruising my knees. Ms. Penny was right—this was much better!

At the cafeteria, I got in line and looked around. There were still lots of kids ahead of me! I started getting frustrated, but then I remembered my plan.

I was prepared.

"'Step two,'" I read. "'If the line is long, just sing a song.'"
I began singing to pass the time.

I made it through *Pinkle, Pinkle, Little Star* and *Mary Had a Pink Ole Lamb*, and was just about finished with *Old PinkDonald* before I realized I was almost at the front of the line.

"Are you singing something?" asked Ethel the lunch lady. I started to answer her, but the cafeteria was so loud she couldn't hear me.

That's when I knew it was time for step three of my plan.

Is the room very noisy from the lunch-eating crowd? Then roll up this plan, and speak up real loud, it said.

I rolled my plan into a megaphone. I put it up to my mouth and asked for a grilled-cheese sandwich and a piece of pie.

"Huh?" said Ethel. Even with a megaphone, she still couldn't hear me!

Hmmm, I thought. She could hear me when I was singing! I know. . . . "May I please have a grilled cheese and a piece of cherry pie?" I sang. This time, Ethel heard me.

"Yes, you may!" Ethel sang back, handing me the cherry pie.

"Here's your grilled cheese," sang the other lunch lady, giving me another plate. "And how about some strawberry milk?" sang the third lunch lady.

"Thank you!" I sang back.

"You are welcome!" sang the three lunch ladies in perfect harmony.

The cafeteria was completely quiet as everyone listened
to them sing. When they finished, everyone clapped and
yelled, "Hooray!"

The whole room filled up with our cheers. The lunch
lady trio took a bow. I sat down and finally got to eat my
cafeteria feast!

Pinkalicious

and the Little Butterfly

Spring had sprung, and the flowers were in bloom!
Mommy said I could pick some on the way to school
to bring to my teacher, Ms. Penny.

I carefully put the flowers on my table. I couldn't wait for Ms. Penny to see my pink bouquet! When Ms. Penny entered the classroom, she was holding a big box filled with twigs and leaves. Alison and I looked at each other in surprise—what was Ms. Penny doing?

"Good morning, class!" Ms. Penny said. "I have a surprise for you." She set the box on her desk and invited us to come take a closer look. I peered into the box and saw . . .

"Ew, worms!" Tiffany shrieked.

"Cool!" Jack said.

Ms. Penny laughed. "They're not worms; they're caterpillars. One day soon, they will turn into beautiful monarch butterflies."

Two of the caterpillars had black, white, and yellow stripes. They were munching on leaves. The third caterpillar was emerald green. He scooted up and down the twig like a tiny race car.

"How can something so small become a colorful butterfly?" I asked.

"With the right food and love, they will!" Ms. Penny promised.

"Would you like to hold a caterpillar?" asked Ms. Penny. I nodded and slipped my pinky into the box. The green one crawled onto my finger and wiggled around my palm. I had the perfect name for him.

"His name is Wiggles," I said.

"Hi, Wiggles," Alison said. "Welcome to our school!"

Ms. Penny saw the flowers I had brought in earlier. "Did you know that caterpillars like to eat milkweed?" she said.

"I brought them for you," I said.

"Well, I think there's enough to share, don't you?" asked Ms. Penny.

I put some milkweed carefully into the caterpillar house. I wasn't sure, but I thought Wiggles was smiling.

Over the next few weeks, I took extra-special care of Wiggles and his friends. I brought them fresh milkweed every day. Alison helped me put it in the cage.

Sometimes I would sing a song to Wiggles about an itsy-bitsy caterpillar climbing up a waterspout.

I even drew pictures of Wiggles in art class. I loved him.

One morning, I came in early to put leaves into the caterpillar house, but Wiggles wasn't there! His friends were also missing.

"Ms. Penny! Ms. Penny!" I cried. "Someone stole the caterpillars!" Ms. Penny hurried over to look into the box, and then she smiled. "They're not stolen. They're still here!" She pointed to three little teardrops hanging from a twig. "Those are chrysalises, and the caterpillars are sleeping inside. In a few days, they will break open. The next time you see the caterpillars, they will look very different!"

Over the next few days, the entire class watched and waited. Lila sharpened her pencil ten times so she could check on the box. Jack scooted his chair closer to it.

I looked at my pictures of Wiggles. I missed my caterpillar.

"Look!" Molly said after lunch. "The chrysalises are moving!" We all hurried over to watch. Soon two orange butterflies sat on a twig . . . but the pink chrysalis didn't move.

Once the butterflies could fly, Ms. Penny lifted the lid of the box and opened the window. The butterflies flew all around the room and then out the window.

I looked at Wiggles's chrysalis. I was worried. Would I ever see my wiggly friend again?

At home that night, I couldn't stop thinking about Wiggles. Were his wings stuck? Was he lonely? Did he have enough food?

I drew a fairy princess riding a magnificent butterfly. Maybe if I showed Wiggles my picture tomorrow, he would come out and fly.

"What's wrong, Pinkalicious?" Daddy said as he entered my room that night.

I told him about Wiggles, and he gave me a hug. "I'm sure Wiggles will have his wings in no time," he said.

Daddy read me an extra bedtime story and fluttered his eyelashes against my cheek.

"That's a butterfly kiss," he said. "It brings good luck."

The next morning, I rushed to school and hurried
over to the box. The last chrysalis had split open,
but there wasn't an orange butterfly in the box. . . .

There was a PINK butterfly!

"Wiggles!" I gasped. Wiggles delicately flapped his
pinkatastic wings. He gently fluttered from the twig to
the flowers.

"You can't be called Wiggles anymore," I said.
"From now on, I am going to call you Flutterby."

When the bell rang for recess, Ms. Penny carefully picked up the box and we went outside. "Pinkalicious, would you like to do the honors?" she asked.

I came forward and gently lifted the lid. Flutterby gracefully flew out of the box. He swooped around me, then flitted onto my head before he soared upward, stretching his new wings.

"Flutterby, my butterfly," I called out to my friend. He dipped his antennae to say good-bye before sailing off into the blue sky.

Pinkalicious

and Aqua, the Mini-Mermaid

Peter and I were going to see our merminnie friend, Aqua, for a special playdate! She was going to show us all her favorite seaside spots.

We headed over to the aquarium, where Aqua lives. When we arrived, we found Aqua in a tank full of colorful creatures.

"Hi, Aqua," I said. "Ready to go?"

"Just a moment," she replied. "I'm almost done teaching this school of fish how to mambo."

While we waited, Peter and I checked out the aquarium.

"Look," I said. "That's a butterfly fish! And this one's called a parrot fish." "I found a frog fish and a toadfish." Peter pointed.

We saw a goatfish, a scorpion fish, and a porcupine fish, too. "Maybe they should call this a zoo-quarium," I said.

At last, Aqua was ready for our adventure. She met us outside. "Let's go this way," she said, motioning toward the ocean.

We scooped up Aqua in my pink bucket and skipped through the surf. Soon we reached a big hole filled with water.

"Welcome to the tide pool," said Aqua. We leaned over the edge and peeked in. There were starfish, clams, and sea plants everywhere! It was like a miniature ocean, perfect for our miniature friend.

"This is my favorite spot to think," said Aqua. "Clams make great listeners."

Peter stepped on something flat and smooth as we walked along the coast. "What's this?" he said.

"Oh," cried Aqua. "A sand dollar! How wonderful!"

Peter's eyes widened. "A sand dollar? Excuse me, Aqua, but I need to borrow this bucket."

Aqua and I relaxed on the shore as Peter hunted for sand dollars. "Should we tell him it's not real money?" Aqua whispered.

"Maybe in a minute," I said.

Just then, we heard a big rumble. "Oh, the waves are loud today," Aqua marveled.

"Actually, that was my tummy," I said. "Excuse me." It was definitely time for a snack.

"I know just the place," said Aqua.

Our merminnie guided us to a grove of palm trees with more coconuts than you could count!

Aqua showed us how to split them in half and sip the milk inside. It was like our own tropical tea party.

"May I offer you a little milk, Aqua?" I said, pouring some into a seashell.

"Why, thank you," Aqua replied. "It goes perfectly with my seaweed sandwich."

After we ate, Aqua said she had one more place to show us. "But this one is a surprise," she said with a smile.

She led us to a cove and told us to close our eyes. We walked very, very slowly. "Now," said Aqua, "look around you."

In the cove was the most beautiful collection of ocean treasure we had ever seen. There were seashells of every shape and color. Pieces of sea glass sparkled in the sunlight.

"This is where I keep all the treasure I find on my sea adventures," said Aqua. "It's my special collection. Do you like it?"

But Peter and I couldn't answer. We were simply speechless.

The three of us sat in the cove and looked out at the ocean. Everything was peaceful and quiet.

Suddenly, Peter stood up. "Uh-oh," he said. "I think we've got company."

Off in the distance, we saw two fins poking out of the water. They were swimming toward us fast.

"Are those sharks?" I asked Aqua. She gulped. "I hope not," she said.

The fins got closer and closer. I was scared. "What are we going to do?" said Peter.

"Maybe they just want to be friends," I said, though I wasn't so sure there was such a thing as a friendly shark.

Just then, the creatures burst out of the water. They weren't sharks at all. They were dolphins. And not only that—they were pink dolphins!

"Of course," said Aqua. "I should have known. Pinkalicious and Peter, meet Sandy and Shelly. They pass through here around this time every year."

"How do you do?" I said, curtsying.

"Thank goodness you aren't sharks!" said Peter.

Sandy and Shelly bobbed their heads and squealed. Then they jumped way up high and did double flips.

"I think they like you," said Aqua. "They're putting on a show!"

Sandy and Shelly leaped and twisted and twirled and splashed. When they were done, they nudged us with their noses.

"They want you to join them," said Aqua.

Peter looked at me. I looked at Peter. A swim with the dolphins? How could we resist?

As the sun began to set, we knew it was time to go home. Sandy and Shelly gave the three of us a ride back to the aquarium.

"Good-bye," we called from the beach as their fins disappeared back into the ocean.

We waved good-bye to Aqua and thanked her for showing us all her favorite spots. "The beach is full of magic," I said, "and you're the most marvelous part."

"Yeah," said Peter. "That's for sure!"

As I lay in bed that night, I could still smell the salty sea air. I made a wish upon a sea star that I'd be back to visit soon.

Pinkalicious

Apples, Apples, Apples!

We were at the Pinkville Orchard.
It was Apple Harvest Day!

Peter and I found the map of the
farm. I read the names of the different
apple trees.

"Pinkawow!" I shouted.
"There's a kind of apple called
Pink Lady!" I couldn't believe it—
a pinkaperfect apple! I had to
find it right away.

Peter and I searched through rows and rows of trees. We found red apples, green apples, giant apples, and tiny apples. But no Pink Ladies.

"Keep looking, Peter," I said. "They've got to be here somewhere!"

"Oh, Pinkalicious," Peter called from behind me. "Look what I found!" I turned around and saw my brother with his arms full of round, rosy apples.

"Pink Ladies for a pink lady?" he said.

Peter and I giggled as we put the apples in our wagon.
"Let's get some more," I said.

We ran back and forth until we filled up the wagon.
"More?" asked Peter. "More!" I answered.

By the time Mommy and Daddy found us, our apple pile
was an apple pyramid of beautiful Pink Ladies.

"Oh dear," Mommy said.

"What are we going to do with all this fruit?" said Daddy.
Peter and I looked at each other. We hadn't thought of that.

We rode home very carefully—and very slowly. Peter and I kept looking back to make sure the apples didn't fall off the wagon.

"Oh dear," said Mommy again. Straight ahead of us was a giant hill. Mommy looked at Daddy. Peter looked at me.

"Uh-oh," I said.

Up, up, up we climbed. We pedaled and pushed our way to the top. At long last, we were almost home. I could see all of Pinkville down below!

I was so excited to get home that I started pedaling faster. "Wait," said Daddy. "Be careful or the apples will—"

Daddy didn't get to finish his sentence. He was interrupted by the sound of rolling apples. The Pink Ladies fell out of the wagon and went flying down the hill!

We tried to catch them, but they were rolling much too fast. In just a few seconds, the streets of Pinkville were covered with fruit.

"Come on," I yelled. "We have to get our apples!"

Peter and Mommy ran in one direction. Daddy and I ran in another. We followed the apples as they tumbled down the street, picking them up one by one.

We searched high and low for our missing Pink Ladies. Mommy and Peter found a bunch that had rolled into the school yard.

Mr. Swizzle had some by the front door of his ice-cream parlor.

I saw three hiding under the rose bushes in Pinkville Park.

Little by little, we gathered up all the Pink Ladies and brought them home. Then we washed them and washed them and washed them some more. Some of them were a little bit bruised, but they were still good enough to eat.

So we ate them. All week, we had apples with every meal.
Apple cake and apple crumble.
Apple sauce and apple cider.

Sliced apples. Diced apples. Dried apples. Fried apples. Even apple ice cream.

By Friday, we had eaten nothing but apples—and we still had many left! It felt like we were never going to finish.

That night, I thought about how we had too many apples and not enough people to eat them. And I thought about how my family had looked for the Pink Lady apples all over town.

That's when I had an idea. Since we couldn't eat all the apples on our own, maybe we could share them with the rest of Pinkville and call it Apple Appreciation Day.

The following Monday, I brought a shiny fresh apple and a whole apple pie to school and gave them to Ms. Penny.

"Thank you, Pinkalicious," she said. "To what do I owe this surprise?"

"It's Apple Appreciation Day," I said. "I appreciate you, Ms. Penny, so you get an applelicious treat! Thank you for being the best teacher ever!"

My friend Alison was out sick, so when I got home Mommy and I went over to her house with a basket of apples.

"I'm sorry you're sick," I said. "Since an apple a day keeps the doctor away, I hope this keeps you healthy for a long, long time!"

Alison giggled. She bit into an apple. "I feel better already!" she said.

Everywhere we went, we handed out apples and apple treats.

Finally, we reached Mr. Swizzle's shop. We gave him a small container of apple ice cream.

"Mr. Swizzle, you spend all day making sweet treats for everyone in Pinkville," I said. "This time, we wanted to make something delicious for you! Happy Apple Appreciation Day!"

Mr. Swizzle took one bite. "This is marvelous. This is excellent. This is positively applelicious!" he said. "What do you call it?"

"Pink Lady Supreme," I said with a smile.

By that evening, we had given away almost all our apples. We had only one left.

"Looks like Apple Appreciation Day was a huge success," said Mommy and Daddy, giving me a big hug.

Then Mommy took the last apple out of the basket. "This one's for you, Pinkalicious," she said as she cut it in half and twisted it open. Inside there was a star.

"A Pink Lady with a star inside," said Daddy. "That sounds like someone I know."

"Thanks for being so generous with the apples and for thinking of other people," said Mommy and Daddy. "You are our star."